THE BARBARIANS' RETURN

MIRCEA DINESCU

The Barbarians' Return

SELECTED POEMS

Translated from the Romanian by
ADAM J. SORKIN & LIDIA VIANU

BLOODAXE BOOKS

First published 2018 by
Bloodaxe Books Ltd,
Eastburn,
South Park,
Hexham,
Northumberland NE46 1BS.

www.bloodaxebooks.com
For further information about Bloodaxe titles
please visit our website or write to
the above address for a catalogue.

Supported using public funding by
**ARTS COUNCIL
ENGLAND**

Cover design: Neil Astley & Pamela Robertson-Pearce.

Printed in Great Britain by Bell & Bain Limited, Glasgow, Scotland, on
acid-free paper sourced from mills with FSC chain of custody certification.

ACKNOWLEDGEMENTS

The poems in this edition have been selected from Mircea Dinescu's Romanian retrospective, *Întoarcerea barbarilor: Versuri libere 2013–1973* (Editura Litera, Bucharest, 2014).

Six of the translations were previously published in the Romanian special issue of *Poem* 4.3-4 (September-December 2016).

The publication of this book was supported by a grant from the Romanian Cultural Insitute, Bucharest.

 INSTITUTUL
CULTURAL
R O M Â N

CONTENTS

A nutshell biography, by the poet himself

Born in a provincial town to a family that belonged to the lumpen-
proletariat and in whose house no book other than a Bible could
be found, it could be said of Mircea Dinescu that he formed him-
self as a poet through photosynthesis: he sounded out on his own
the music of sunspots. At sixteen, he made his totally unexpected
début in the literary press. Like a most stubborn mule, he was
burdened by literary critics with the title of the *enfant terrible* of
Romanian literature, and this continued until the poet was in his 40s.
Instead of conforming to the comfortable system of the Communist
bourgeoisie that had already honoured him with the venerable
Prize of the Academy of the Socialist Republic of Romania, he
kicked over the milk bucket with his hoof, as Romanians often
say: he objected openly and irreverently to the former shoemaker
who had become the President of the country, Nicolae Ceaușescu,
and who was doing his best to build a Romania according to the
model of Mao Zedong's cultural revolution.

In an interview that appeared on 17 March 1989 in the Parisian
newspaper *Libération*, Dinescu spoke of Romania as 'a country
where border guards stand with their guns turned against the
citizens who longed to defect to the rotten West, a country where
"the most beloved son of the people" actually showed his peasants
how to hold a spade, explained to his workers which end of a nail
should be driven, and taught all his authors how to write from left
to right, a country wherein truth walked about with a shattered
skull, a country inhabited by failed suicides who could not even
set themselves on fire in the public square because of the dire
shortage of boxes of matches and who could not hang themselves
either, for lack of ropes and soap.'

Placed under house arrest for the offence of *lèse-majesté*, Dinescu
was liberated nine months later, on 22 December, by the large
crowd of Romanians who had filled the streets of Bucharest in
revolt and who carried him triumphantly to the national television
building. There, reversing the pattern of the late Fidel Castro, the

poet announced with actor Ion Caramitru to everyone who was watching that the dictator had fled. At that moment, something took place that Karl Marx had never imagined in his blackest and deepest nightmares: the country changed from communist to capitalist.

The revolution tried to devour its own progeny, so to speak, but Dinescu saved himself by hiding in the pages of a satirical political magazine, and he kept writing pamphlets that appealed to large audiences.

In the year 2003, in an issue dedicated to Heroes, the review *Times Europe* nominated Mircea Dinescu under the category of Hate Busters. On that occasion, this particular 'hero' stated that, had he been Japanese, he would have committed hara-kiri when Eastern European society eagerly became a mock consumerist society. But since he wasn't Japanese, the poet committed an extended version of that hara-kiri: he mocked at history by starring in a gastronomic TV show entitled *Politics and Delicatessen*, by raising goats on his farm along the banks of the Danube, by making fine wines in his personal winery in the hills of Oltenia, where the farmer and the chef have eclipsed the poet.

Currently, Dinescu owns a house in a former agricultural port on the Danube that he has transformed into a cultural harbour. Nowadays, he sits on the river bank, waiting patiently to see the bodies of all his imaginary enemies float by.

THE BARBARIANS' RETURN

Discourse upon Europe's reception of an eastern country

In church
the thief, ashamed, hides his hands in the bishop's pocket
so the good Lord shouldn't see them.
The peasant shouts at his big-hoofed son
to put away the boots he left by the shed
for guests are coming
and, what the hell, we've got our national pride,
Japanese tourists are on the way
with their tiny sparrow-like feet
pitter-patter, pitter-patter
to peck at wheat, sunflowers, Van Gogh's eyes.
Suddenly
it's tenderness hour in the municipal hospital
and the drunk admitted for drying out
fondles the medicinal spirits the nurse forgot on the nightstand
calling it 'violet courage',
'creeping death', 'corpse reviver',
then he throws a window open wide and screams,
'Welcome, consumer society,
come, kill us too
like all the rest,
polish our kidney stones into lucky dice.
From now on, we won't call the arse *comrade* but *sir*,
starting tomorrow it's going to be harder to get me out of the pub
than to get Shakespeare out of the Encyclopaedia Britannica.'

The fiancé's hesitation

There's a hole in the floor:
neither capitalist nor communist,
it's a partyless hole.
It's so transparent
it could become an Academy member,
so virtuous
I almost could marry it.
But I keep thinking
before long
it's going to cheat on me with a mouse.

Letter to Václav Havel, thrown into the wastepaper basket

Havel, please get thee to a monastery
I just can't get used to the idea that
the eagle
works for the sanitation department.
Revolutions have eaten their offspring,
dissidents are unemployed,
protesters stand contritely
in line at McDonald's,
only you've managed to make a few posh suits
out of that historical velvet
for which I envy you.
I envy you because in Prague
marijuana's cheaper than bread
and along the bridges teenagers
lick the crack from postage stamps.
I envy your being granted
an *honoris causa*
every three days;
my mother, too, hoped I'd become
a doctor of letters so as to cure her lungs
– I never have.
I envy you for having taken back your market stalls;
Ezra Pound dreamt of having a small tobacconist's shop
– he never did.
When the communion bread mildews
you're supposed to bury it very deep
so that neither rats nor dogs can dig it out,
however when there's this inflation of angels,
who'd mind a rat with wings,
a dog in flight?
But we've something worse
that worries me.
Cars continue to be
five times heavier than they should be

and can hardly drive themselves along.
Cows die of starvation
just three hundred metres from the railway station
where wheat forgotten on the abandoned tracks
sticks its green tongue out at travellers
through carriage roofs.
Our new society gasps,
pants with bent back under everlasting clerks.
The watchmen, unwatched,
steal everything.
The poor man's bread – the only luck he knows –
drops as shit as it always has,
he gets an erection during the church service,
and firemen climb on the roof of his house
on his wedding night.
How can I make sense of things
when communists play hide and seek in the church
and, in a fit of bourgeois philanthropy,
they're ready to hire me
to rewrite as artistically as I can
the theories and laws of *Das Kapital*?
How can I make sense of things when the barbarians
no longer reach the gates of Rome
because they're arrested at the Czech border?
Make sense of what? That the angel's more readable than Marx?
Of course I feel like crying out
like the loony at the Louvre,
'Give me a knife, so I can cut my Christmas bacon-rind
from Brueghel the Elder, Velázquez or Goya,
hand me a country
and you'll soon be drinking the police tea
prophesied by Mandelstam.'
O, hypocrite lecteur, mon semblable, mon frère,
don't lose heart,
don't lose heart,
don't lose heart, but do take care when you cross the street
lest an ambulance run you over.

Right to free circulation

Just as Shakespeare can take the liberty
to blow his nose in Desdemona's handkerchief,
I want to play toreador to the bull that ravished Europa,
to slay it by jabbing my pen with invisible ink
between its horns
so I may marry the girl for convenience,
so I may be granted French citizenship, Belgian or German
like the bum I met twenty years ago
on the Novosibirsk train
who dreamt he'd flee from the wild East to Israel,
marry an old Jewish woman,
considering her not a luxury but a means of transportation,
without any Christian complexes,
since, ultimately
Jesus is the fruit of a *ménage à trois*.

Pest control

A guy comes
with a stinking canister on his back.
'Who are those wretched, shrunken creatures
hidden behind the furniture?'
Only my parents, who survived World War I
and World War II.
But now it's going to be a lot harder.

The barbarians' return

In the evening
when the Barbarians return from the West mounted on concepts,
sent as emissaries of huge salami factories,
don't ask about their horses,
put out the fire
stuff your mouth with embers
fill your memory with ashes
and head for the Himalayas with your trumpet
cultivate avalanches
change your sex, name or Linnaean kingdom
mingle with a gaggle of geese
go honk-honk and seize
the moment – be an Eskimo
when the green ice-nerve in Antarctica
slowly relaxes
propose to the plump lascivious seal
lick honey from the federal administrator's fingers
or simply stand meekly and listen to
the howl of the crude oil of the locomotive
giving birth in the middle of the field without a midwife
to a procession of tiny luminous creatures.

Drunk with Marx

Dear old Marx, in these parts
you'll soon be shaved and sent for re-education.
Everything's your fault,
even the fact that Eastern cows
put to pasture by the railway tracks
think of themselves as carriages and no longer give milk.
Better that this town fall into the merchants' hands
that it no longer reek of rhetoric
that the brewers, the pastrami-makers, and the dairy farmers
debate the dialectics of fermented barley
and cheese curds.
At present, peasants would sooner scythe the green cuttlefish on
      the punks' heads,
and the new philosophers, suspecting that you're dead,
delude themselves that they're arguing with you.
They just can't smell the barmy yeast
as society swells,
putting into use the alembic
through which the heated Cohn-Bendit
is made to condense into an obedient functionary.
Even a thoroughly ordinary guy like me
leaves syntax and logic behind like a slug
and dreams of that strange stomach disease
where you get drunk on a slice of bread.
Here, taste it!
We're on our way:
in Berlin the clocks have gone crackers.

Interview

For us life's good in the countryside, it's beautiful,
our principles have grown rather old
but drinking medicinal spirits strained through bread rejuvenates us
and even the doctor's assistant recommends it 'for internal use'.
Here the church pronaos has been rededicated to agriculture
the pig has chewed up the baby left in the trough
(no problem, both belonged to the state)
really life in the countryside's good,
little children hold their mugs under the TV possibly it'll give milk
according to the radio the harvest was a great success
even the fields we still have to finish
really life's good for us in the countryside, it's fine it's super
if you can buy your eggs in the city
if the salami factory doesn't
cast its eye on the horses.
For us life's very good in the countryside
the firemen set fire to houses it's beautiful
the tractor does its ploughing between some of us and the rest
between some of us and the rest a deep furrow
it's good it's beautiful.

Epistle about accepting reality
with a somewhat metaphysical postscript

How can one man's anger
despoil such a great acreage of farmland,
and his petty chill spread like ivy over blast furnaces?
Look, you docs of the Ostrich Academy,
there's not enough sand for us to hide our heads,
look, Magister Procopius, we too can scribble
on the skin of a calf yet unborn.

Post Scriptum. It's with deep sorrow
Oh Lord that we heard the rumour
of your allowing the Pope's hiccup
to toll the Vatican bells.

Short ceremony at the interment of a submarine from between the two world wars

Ever since birth
I put my whimpers
at the service of artists destroyed by starvation.
In a bottle of booze
I could have turned my back on you forever
but I don't know along what obscure paths
doubt dogged my footsteps
so here I am today like that shipboard fool
praying 'God, give me a ship'
or like a stonyhearted midwife
at the painless delivery of a stevedore from a priest.
With a thread from Ariadne's socks in hand
I vanish into an army greatcoat
looking at the world through a pair of boots
as if through the wrong end of two periscopes.

Autumn show

Imagination costs nothing
who know this better than God-the-painter
in September
when he takes advantage of the poor man's dampness and cold
to open an impressionist exhibit on the moist wall:
small framed spots, a sodden voluptuousness that inspires Manet
and of which neither priest nor ceremony-loving mayor have any idea
otherwise, it goes without saying, a ribbon would be cut
speeches intoned champagne set bubbling
and critics would gnaw on pink bone,
here at the poor man's wall
where God's rheumatic hand
perfects his work.

Futile attempt to make a dinosaur move

A piece of bread fallen under the table
bored itself one fine day inventing mice and cockroaches,
only my solitude invents nothing.
With a nausea devoid of imagination
like a myopic naturalist
I try from one odd glove to reconstitute
the prehistoric animal of our love:
whoo whoo, it goes, whirr whirr
chug chug, it rumbles like a sputnik of peace,
thump thump vroom vroom vroom vroom
vroom vroom vroom vroom vroom vroom
hissss...

Hens

In a castle turned into a chicken farm
we caroused till dawn with the caretaker and the watchman
we drank wine made from red beet root – and didn't give a damn
white wine made from rotten fence rails – and didn't give a damn
the hens had an undeveloped political consciousness
they cackled softly and closed their eyes to what was going on
pecked at the impasto of the paintings
scratched at Brueghel the Elder
cackled inside the clavier
laid eggs in the Biedermeier
(from their gizzards Savonarola made himself a stylish soutane)
we were happy
ready to set forth on a hunt for lions
armed with flypaper,
revolution smelled like a baked potato
loudspeakers replaced art
there were lamps that shed darkness
and letterboxes no one opened any longer
we too cackled softly
and closed our eyes to what was going on.

Fictionalised story of a failed suicide

Amid the '47 famine and worries,
I was almost born
but my smiling mother gave birth to my blind brother.

I almost had to eat mulberries
but the wind scattered them into the neighbours' yard.

The war was colder than beer.

I almost made it with a girl
but another with prior rights took my place.

When I competed with myself I came out second.

Only after I threw myself into the Seine
did I remember – how embarrassing! – that I could swim.

Autopsy of an angel

As you cry in a corner of the shed
your tears catch in the spider webs
and the spiders marvel at those bitter flies.

A maidservant from a past century
happily combs her hair on the threshold of a house
collapsed just yesterday in an earthquake.

There's nothing you can do
for the crazy child hidden in the thicket
who exhales sparks and soot through his mouth
like a steamboat.
He's the very likeness of an egg
with a halo inside.
If you touch the rosebush beside him
you'd be electrocuted.

Nature's democracy

In March dustbins explode
splattering the neorealist darkness
with flame-red cats.
The town boils below their greedy phosphorus
a kiss smelling saccharine like brimstone,
pregnant women might suddenly flow into the room
but for the heavy sandbags
grumbling in front of the TV
blowing into the eternal soup.
Swarms of butterflies slip under girls' skirts
and my hand falls heavy with pollen.
A tiny thermoelectric generator installed in fools' mouths
now reaches full productivity
(poor and lazy, I'm not the least afraid).
A child pisses on the church steeple
and God welcomes the warm jet
like a rheumatic heel that needs soothing.
A rotten potato tossed on the empty plot of ground
shows its little green penis
like a sign of nature's democracy.

Strolling player

My God – I was born
red with fury
bawling in a language known to no one
burdened with lightning and bombast like a great actor
and I will vanish
palsied in the face of death and carrying a tray
piled high with stage fright
like an amateur on the provincial boards
the prompter smothered inside his breast.

One factory summons another

A hundred women run away every month
from the workers' dorms at the silk factory
the barking of the weaving looms echoes in the emptiness
the production schedule creeps away across the floor
unimplemented
the manager's hair turns grey
the telephone screams
green with fury the dollars go whoosh back to the West,
slogans shout their message in larger and larger letters
meetings get held at higher and higher temperatures
lorries carry in girls from nearby villages
who get trained as they work
but every month a hundred women run away
aroused like bulls by the sight of red silk
in a corrida minus blood and toreadors.
If only the bulldozers would hurry this way
and level the ground,
the masons and ironsmiths
the drivers who wolf-whistle between their teeth
the grizzled bums the building-site artists,
then the conveyor belts would rumble
the Siemens Martin ovens croon
there'd be a perfume of crude oil and coal
to calm the girls,
hand in hand
silk and cast iron
one factory beside another.

The avalanche

At 9 o'clock in the morning on the 11th of November
I had a date
with a young avalanche
in the Himalayas
on the gentlest of slopes.
It would have been love at first sight
but by the time my passport was issued
by the time I'd declared all my relatives
by the time I'd packed my suitcases
by the time I'd bought my ticket
by the time I'd been patted down by the customs officers
by the time I'd been sniffed all over by the detectors,
at 9:15
spurned and hysterical
the avalanche ran away down the slope with a Greek and two Japanese...

God should abolish the institutions of sadness
those that fight against love
against love and death.

Winter indulgence

God protect me from those who know what's best for me
the smiling fellows
eager to inform in an instant
the priest with a tape-recorder under his cassock
the bedcovers you can't pull up without saying
good evening
the dictators who get tangled up in harp strings
those enraged at their own people
now as winter draws near
we've neither high walls
nor geese on the Capitol
just an enormous supply of indulgence and fear

The hypocritical dead

Literature, what are you really good for?
You confuse young provincial blockheads
you seat the paper supplier
at a table beside someone with a bellyful of letters,
you place golden lice in the bohemian's long hair
and the tricolour on the academician's breast,
but you can't make water sweet to the drowned
nor melt the leper's snow
nor fatten up the poor.
When God's accountants arrive
with their registers to weigh contrition
you against pigeons
you against doves
you against the small birds
you climb the city hall tower
and throw
a fistful of millet to the angels of the apocalypse
but in the inner courtyard you fail to see
the criminal as he tickles his victim
and the base dead man as he laughs to humour you
the dead accomplice laughs
the purposelessly dead
the hypocritical dead of our district.

A day without a sandwich

Where two streets bump into each other like fools
and you yourself bump into the blind man with a harmonica,
if you have a little luck he smiles a guilty smile
and blows *The Waves of the Danube* in your ears,
but don't be upset, quick, give him his coin
if you want to get away with your collar in one piece
or keep your chin out of his greasy fingers
or avoid being firmly stomped on by his boot
as if he knew something about your fictionalised biography
quick give him his coin
be glad you escaped unscathed
forget about a sandwich for today.

The sad hijacking of the suicide

Oh Lord, you've left behind in man
the gleam of your silver instrument
like an absentminded surgeon
who stitches scalpel and forceps inside his patient.
Why else this aimless despair
the irony of these borrowed tears?
Electrocuted by an angel, the epileptic
remains pregnant
but who'll be the midwife to deliver the reverie from his brow.

Because of melancholy the suicide
throws himself down from Notre Dame Cathedral
and crushes a child in his fall.
Who doomed him in his flight to become a child murderer?
It's not for nothing that bums have written on walls,
'place to bang your head',
thus offering you one last chance to make sure
whether this death's rightly yours,
whether this death's a strictly personal affair.

A tune by Armstrong

Evenings when bands begin to kill
and seven thousand drunks set sail for America on waves of beer
the kangaroo in the pregnant virgin's nightmare
will knock on your door
his pouch stuffed with threatening letters.
In order to calm your imagination, go out into the street
you're an invalid for whom everything's allowed out of pity and
     disgust,
like a cooled volcano,
your throat gagged with newspapers and bottles,
surprise the tourists tonight
and play a tune by Armstrong
on your lava trumpet.

Short extract from the secret files of the 100 Years' War

The importance of the little mouse in the 100 Years' War
when knights had set forth on a mission
is dismissed out of hand by the ignorant chroniclers of the age
if not (undeservedly) overlooked:
'What you had to do was to scramble across the floor
and the princess all atremble threw herself
into the stable boy's arms
the governess under the tolerant priest's cloak
the cook in the basket of carrots, oh me oh my...
Your squeaks brought into this world
several dozen noblemen with fresh blood
merchants and geniuses
inventors and innumerable cutpurses,
nature's poor pretext
commonsense symbol
tool of democracy on earth.'

Common cheek

I counted 71 feet in the packed metro
(the cripple was among them)
but, Lord God,
no left foot seemed brother to the right
mud had vanquished the strength of the tannery
the shoe looked bedraggled
the boot crumpled
the galosh pouting.
71 honest feet, oh God,
and a common cheek
expressive of nothing.

Bach

Johann Sebastian Bach, aren't you tired of carrying on your back
for three hundred years
the corpse of the polyphonic ox from the lofty organ?
On our children's bread
you spread church honey, steeple honey.
Aren't you tired of believing that the angel's to come
with his angelic toolkit and repair our sins?
Because of you spring's steward got drunk
and lost his keys.
Never mind. The groves must remain unlocked
and plum blossoms eternally rain down upon us.

Winter diary at the *Pontus Euxinus*
(The Year 17 AD)

I hope to pass away in a grocer's shop
in a light coat, delicate as tea,
in my small patch of the south near the Danube's mouth,
among stacks of fragrant boxes...
The merchant is kind and tells me
the story of the monkey found in a bale of St John's bread
who died trying to appreciate the taste of Scythian snow.
It's an exemplum with a rather sad point
but in Rome I know a few people
who'd be happy to hear it.

The death of Sunday

A Monday like any other Monday
but on Tuesday following a snail's slime
I came across the senile crocodile,
and the bailiff harnessed to a gig,
water tasted of incense and wooden planks
the miller's servant-maid puffed out with yeast
and a rake gathered the peasants asleep on the threshing ground
the caravan came
silent films loosed my tongue
I shouted to the crocodile to crawl into a snail shell
I whistled to the horse lost in calculations
I groped for the corpse dumped down the well,
but the priest sang, the mayor gabbed, the sergeant thought thoughts
and the town was as happy as a thresher with all the peasants in its
     belly
on Wednesday the war was over
on Thursday electrification began
on Friday lamps raised questions
on Saturday darkness fell
and on Sunday you could no longer see, no longer see.

Jericho waltz

Don't lose heart, blow the trumpet of death
the way a pensioner blows into hot soup
find new variations
like a jazz singer faced with Jericho
play until the guards drive you away with stones
because tourists are coming
the little frog's eyes must be painted in a hurry
Jesus's seven hundred shrouds must be well starched
tourists are coming starved for tragedy
and the fresh plaster hasn't yet dried on the walls.
If you can imagine it,
a priest astride reality
or in the warm nest of a provincial publishing house,
the bird of paradise brooding over a Mark Twain
then don't lose heart
blow into the rusty funnel
until the walls begin to waltz
in the name of the Father, and of the Son, and of the Holy Ghost.
Amen.

Birth of a definition

Selling the skins of brood hens at the mouth of the Labyrinth
just like Borges
who in derision was appointed inspector of poultry at
the Buenos Aires market
and taking yourself seriously
as if you were tidying up eagle cotes,
as if you'd just set a colony of pelicans in order.
You need to maintain a certain degree of confusion
like the connection between pickpocket and kangaroo,
otherwise an excess of reality can make the poor reporter feel sick
and the literary critic vituperate against the sea
for being too manneristic...
This is what I dare call life:
the fertile agony of objects
to become what they cannot be.

The prayer of the child fallen into a bull

In September when the angel's gall bladder bursts
(the angel lies in pain without being able to die)
come filled with promise like a chemist's
with grace and a swarm of wasps beguiling you under the skin
and comb our tangled bones
sift our salt through your sieves
and our water
and the iron nose-ring of the gelded bull
which grows in our body overwhelming us.

Guernica

Wherever they pass by with their damp imagination
lichens and reindeer bloom,
disgusted lamps swallow their own wicks
as wise men their tongues facing the tyrant,
but the gods born in the humming of cafés
vanish one night on the freight trains of the south
condemned without witnesses to a twisted, artificial mythology
to search for flute seeds from who knows which marsh reeds,
to dig their own graves in the rain
and make a passage to the sea ...
Oh vulnerable, vulnerable gods,
death is a homeland without newspapers.

Is it guilt you want to know about?

Favourable circumstances
that inexplicable mystery in old Joseph's house
and pity for the Magi, 'Behold, a virgin shall be with child,
and shall bring forth a son, and they shall call his name Emmanuel,'
exhausted from doubt and signs (blood-red the water in the wine
    thief)
their weariness had to bear fruit,
their weariness bore fruit...

Out of shame I invented my own halo,
out of despair levitation, the whole extravaganza,
it wasn't easy to walk on water,
however I satisfied a crowd with three fish
for I had no doubt their hunger wasn't in their stomachs but in
    their ears.
The autumn of the Empire was approaching
(Barbarians whooped and in Rome pine trees and courtesans kept
    shaking)
and to the young,
my naive friends,
I revealed the breach in provincial towns
through which they'd crept towards death.
I once believed
or at least had a hunch
that inside man
was an ancient watch-like mechanism
when you wound it the right way it sang.

Musical soirée

My brother went blind on a July evening.
In the crucible of the nitrogen plant, shameless Nature
stripped away her plastic stocking.
I wanted to give him my eyes
to help him overcome the shame of his having to feel his way
all over again.
There was no sign from gods
no subtle gift from destiny
as in Homer or Borges
but the consequence of his birth
in the manger of cold war
when my unschooled mother
couldn't find in the entire province
a common eye medicine.
These days, the enterprising petty racketeer
flies carnations to the North
but on the other side of the hill
the peasant smothers his calf with a plastic sack
and buries it secretly
thus free of his obligation
of giving it to the State.
My brother knows none of these things.
He hears the sweet hissing of nitrogen
and feels how tightly the musical stocking
clings to the town's skull.

Death climbed to the roof of our house

Death climbed to the roof of our house
she sets tiles and patches the flue
whispers a word to the dough and the proud dough believes and
     grows
the newly dropped calf
licks
the warm salt from the sweat of her palm
and the bagpipe holding my breath inside its belly
seems filled with yet unpiped fragrances
death climbed to the roof of our house
death climbed to the roof of our house.

Don't worry

What can even prophets do?
They drink sour beer and their revolt rises a semitone
until the buses come
to drive them to showplace villages
to bathe them in reality: plop!

Seated at long tables
fuddled and flushed red from wine
an arm around the mayor's shoulders, another around the police
    chief, they sing
and lead sinks heavily to their feet
but it will surface much more lightly in the morning papers.

Don't worry
I share their colour too
I join in
don't worry,
I haven't seen the angels stacked in the shed
or the aurora hammered in place on a nail, don't worry.
At the village festival
at folk weddings
I'll stick an accordion's bellows to my typewriter
I'll do my duty, don't worry,
I'll sing too, just don't worry
even in the name of good Lord! nonsense, don't worry.

Give the kitchen table a chance

Shipwrecked and going under with the Sèvres bowl in my arms
chanting in the ancient language of the Incas
(like all the shipwrecked, I've grown ridiculously cultivated)
with the Sèvres rock in my arms
I cry out and cry out again
give the kitchen table a chance
let her marry me
or at least the grocer's chopping block
or the consumptive fence rail…
Dear God, the care with which you keep your fruit
far from lovers' lips at sea.

Pocket song

Death was younger than me
but some people made her toys
and taught her to grow up faster.
I know these are commonplaces that fatten up mankind
I know knife-grinders who hone principles
but let Madame Dior dream of fur collars
and inevitably the taiga fills with traps and blood.
You
who are used to finding the hermit's horseradish
at the supermarket on the corner
I've the impression you'd brought oranges on a visit to a deathbed,
for in this street God loves only up to number 24,
where Muslim homes begin and those of uncertain nationality
Romanians, Bulgarians, Albanians
even the Polish cavalry
with swords brandished before a Primark
just as before the Russians.
What teacher could school us
in the tinkling of coins
so we can learn it by heart
hidden deep inside the pocket
in hopes that History
never counts its change.

Meekly

Meekly I'll retire to the cat colony in the southern ocean
near the phosphor of their unrevealing eyes
I'll watch ships sink
catch fish after fish
and yowl with delight like a randy old codger
stalking prepubescent girls among the high-rise flats
no longer would I hear jackhammers separating lovers in hospitals
or the hiss of gas through the meter
or the four o'clock siren
I'll gobble down fish after fish till my life's last moment
licking salt and days off my claws
at night
among tiny furs crackling with static
attracting bewildered angels
like scraps of paper in love with ebonite.

Let me tell you: the scoundrel's lost his sense of honour

The scoundrel's lost his sense of honour
and withdrawn his green tongue from among the leaves
his tongue as sticky as a church
where in its radar the bewildered angel
falls wounded by the bishop's eloquence.

The kind scoundrel
the decent scoundrel
compliments the cripple whose legs are knotted
like an infinity sign
grazes on the flowers at the widow's door
cocks a gigantic ear high above the city
abolishes censorship
and allows the dead to speak
the future is yours, he proclaims
the future and the sparrows on the fence
even though what you call coffee's only roasted barley
even though an egg in a shop window seems exotic
you have a right
you have a right
(a right and a left)
left right left right
right
the future belongs to the cripple
whose legs are knotted like an infinity sign.

After all, it takes so little to be happy
like a breath of air for a drowning man
a miniature ship for a sailor.
After seven years the bones of the dead should be washed with wine
except that wine has now left for America
the little ewe-lamb bleats its baa baa in Beirut
and our left sock is now on Ivan's foot.

You dance the *sîrba* round and round the slaughterhouse cart
and don't hear what I'm shouting to you
that the scoundrel's turning dishonest
that the scoundrel's turning kind
that the scoundrel's decent, just one of the boys.

The age of gods

Like the mad swineherd on the plateau of Iran
with his herd of pigs, an absurd trade,
chanting to horrified anchorites
that pork is the very best fish,
whither, rosewood, do you go,
my merry and illiterate flesh?
Can't you feel spring with its unchristianised germs
sniff around you as if you were a holy church,
while the Master John the Baptist
exceeds the production quota at the reservoir dam
and allows philosophers to gather
in the tailrace
under torrents
under the pressure of matter?
What a crowd in this body, oh my God,
where bones greet one another in the evening,
and the mannerism,
irony *dulcissima*,
seeing April the conjurer a hundred times
and calling it the age of gods...
Whither, rosewood, do you go,
my merry and illiterate flesh?

Speech against revolt

Revolt hasn't won me large spreads of land
unproductive and hysterical
at night it crept under my blanket with me
by day it electrocuted me in the field,
give me a watermelon to prop myself against
give me a speeding train to lean on
because shamelessly I get hungry on the stake
and I've an ammunition belt in place of a spine
woof woof I'm the dog and the hunter
I'm the native chased through the marshes
I no longer love myself so I'm growing old
God's a bottomless pocket
solitude eternally manufactures
copycat amateur suicides
I want to be born but my mother says she's had enough
I want to cry but others cry with greater talent,
give me a watermelon to prop myself against
give me a speeding train to lean on.

Lord, who are they?

Lord, who are these nappy inspectors
obsessed by forbidden doors
always ready to confuse my childhood with a factory
and my blanket with the North Station?!
They give the key of parable a little turn
and the prodigal son falls again into the clutches of the police
they know how to breathe
so as to extinguish my lamp
when the tide deposits lunatics upon the shore
the water pipes croon to the Bedouin
and cry out that we should all belly-dance.

The discovery of America

Give yourself a chance, Columbus of garbage,
reader of cockroaches,
when the world's made new
you'll serve as quiet witness
that
a lemon a bottle a shoe a trumpet
a knife a food tin a potato a newspaper
and watermelon rind

are not the same thing as

watermelon rind sailing through the Bosphorus of the ants
a newspaper with amnesia
a potato in frayed socks
a food tin rusting from a child's tears
a knife excommunicated between an onion and the Pope
a trumpet getting old on top of the manhole cover
a shoe that has a hole with a view of the sea
a bottle empty of meaning
an hysterical lemon...

Ship's log

Sick of lighthouses in the manger of the Balkans
where the sea ripples and in the bodega's loo
you can make a ship from a fence rail
you can be a merchant if you've just a capful of seeds.
A bank note for a hundred will do the trick
and legal papers, either Turkish or Greek:
Ibrahim, Kazaluki or Ianis,
only out at sea can you know your real name.
Europe is in the ship over there. Loudly shout ahoy!
The gramophone in the harbour licks up the foam.
The day slides along the knife blade
and isn't cut off.

Seven drawers

She combs her hair in the evening
and a cloud of electric bees settles in her hair:
a silken chair
wherein a happy man
will be executed by electrocution.

*

A ship creaks and sinks
under the weight of tired butterflies
that have swarmed on its masts.

*

It's enough to give the pyramid a tickle
and the mummy in nappies
bursts out into giggles.

*

Saturday nights
the sea shamelessly unzips its fly.

*

Free crude oil bubbles up in the taiga,
and like an inside-out glove
you're compelled to reveal all
before the lamp.

*

An electric hydropower plant blown high in the air
by the frenzied fish spawning.

*

I wish I had a light pirogue
I'd carry seeds and myrrh to the mouth of the river
among the herons reeds and natives
cup my hands to my mouth and cry whoo whoo
in an old Indian dialect
then whoo whoo the answer would recoil
from the speakers installed along the shore.

Titanic waltz

Speculator of my own death
smuggler with his trunks full of coughs
my bones ring: jingle-jangle
the monks of gastric juice set forth to beg
in big airports
in basements
in railway stations
I'm a sort of cultural ambassador
with holes in my pockets
an overweary wasp buzzing poems
a sunken ship leaving no trace
not even the hint of a waltz
I pray
before the sandwich vending machine
at the clink of the coins
for my little provincial town to drop down
between two slices of bread
jingle-jangle
behind the currency exchange office
in a gleaming WC
I deposit the gold bars of my bladder
(hey there, God of poor poets
where the hell do you hang out?)
followed ever since birth by this iceberg wadded with cotton wool
transistorised god first swallowing my name
staring at me with all many decks
crushing me with all its wheels at once
on a high wave of newspapers
under the high wave of newspapers
jingle-jangle.

Walls

Foolish illusion:
you surround yourself with walls
yet suddenly
feel free.

Manuscript found in a lamp chimney

In the letterbox a cold pair of scissors that cut fingers off
has made its nest.

On the metropolitan church hill there are shop windows
but no shops.

At the tram stop a midget is walking his Philips hump
waiting for gulls.

Cheap unrestricted death is available
but
fuel, paper and God are quite scarce.

If fools could be eaten
there'd no longer be queues at the butcher shops
for intellectuals.

Brief report in support of Romanian language teachers who need more classes each week

In summer he supervises pupils in practical mechanics
in autumn he watches over them in corn-fields
in winter he shovels the snow in front of the school
in spring he sings at the village cultural center
the great shy Romanian teacher
a skilled worker in the Sadoveanu and Tudor Arghezi factories
dressed in a light smock of words he finds a small space
among rulers and logarithms
among saws and lathes
and barely has time to teach his pupils that H_2O
was formerly called water by their ancestors
that it's more natural to say 'good afternoon' than to say radical of 14
and then explain to the pupil Bujie, Ion,
that HPB does not stand for a manufacturer
but for Hortensia Papada-Bengescu herself
that in the past we never had time to build pyramids
and so we had to entomb our pharaohs in folklore
that the Romanian Language is rustless... Stop!
H_2O again, radical of 14, HPB,
Romanian class is over
and we meet again in a week.

Endless Sunday

Give me three absurd masts tonight
I'm the district's transatlantic ocean liner
I'm the fog-dog blinded by lighthouses
stoned by celebrities
kissed by drunkards
baited with bacon by bums.
Here boredom replaces the sea
the shrivelled god without papers
will be killed by common sense at dawn,
here lovers seal themselves up as in a food tin
here old people are plastered over in walls
here only my coughing is sincere
here a zephyr of rumours brings
a zest for life amidst garbage:
football matches upset families
the gramophone's mooing is heard everywhere
spring seems to knock on windows
with its greenfly's fingers...
When all's said and done, I doubt you
until my bitter lips touch yours.

The artist's blessed sleep

Between the roars of optimism factories
and the theory of the perils of idleness
reach a hand out towards a poetry book
and get yourselves a cheap shave
eat its edible covers during a break
strew a few pages among the beetroots
until they are dyed red,
and since the author has nowhere he can sleep
hurry and make his bed inside the barrel:
'Hey, love, the rain won't reach you there,
you won't have a care,
the rifle will be cocked and wake you at dawn.'

The terror of common sense

In my predisposition to consider things
from an unfavourable viewpoint
I'm beginning to believe that the gods buoyed up by a tide of beer
reach us at the table where we slander
their quite possibly impossible existence
until they disappear down to hell on expensive bicycles, all smiles.
Digestible reality:
I walk along the beach
and instead of water I find a notice
the sea is forbidden,
and because of a swarm of fierce wasps
chasing a car on the highway
and because those who were once bound upon the stake
now are required to supply their own wood
what's left for me is to ask
how's your family?
has your cancer spread?
do you enjoy your liberty?
yes you, common man,
a brick half eaten away at the temple
half in the decayed house,
you who place your hope in the milk bottle left on the threshold
office clerk railway worker match-seller
prophet of the timetable of the trams
you rebel against the meter reader
and fail to believe a whale can create an ocean
in public squares
and you've no idea whether you should call the police or an
        ambulance
when from my throat there gushes
a dazzling jet
of happiness or of blood.

How the natives on the reservation
were deprived of the right to travel

A crocodile who'd more than his fill
of native flesh
decided to join the campaign
for their preservation:
with a trader's help he sold his skin
bought top-quality barbed wire
and fenced the reservation so efficiently
that today
crocodiles can no longer get to the natives
but the natives are no longer free to travel to America
in a crocodile's belly.

The door

While you lie on the shore of the dark water
you feel the fly of summer as it buzzes about you
and it's not hard to decipher its message:
remember that you're lugging a corpse on your back.
A ferocious steamboat suddenly goes up the Danube
its joints groaning like an empire,
dragging behind it forests and bridges
herds and houses
church steeples
stuck like snails to the hull,
a steamboat propelled onward
by a natural yet absurd law,
its belly full of peasant children
to be deposited like spawn at the river's source.

Awakened by the splash of a bottle
thrown by a drunkard into the river
or by the sugar factory's whistle
you return to your narrow room in silence
and try to make something out of nothing
glue a frame to a painting
whose painter will never be born
or perhaps
attach a doorknob to a wall
where there never was a door.

Doctor's advice

Tragedies can't stand much heat
the iceberg that struck the Titanic
met its lamentable demise near British Guiana
in the governor's glass of scotch.
The governor himself melted
between two hot stages of History.

Better head north, dictators, head north
to earn your doctorate in cold with honours.

At your disposal

Misfortune saunters around the neighbourhood in my orange shirt
my friends greet it absentmindedly
but I'm the milker of those zeppelins drawn high into the air
between the two world wars,
and I reply by clanging my buckets above the angry mob
who keep shouting, pointing a finger and swearing at me,
'that bloke's running away from reality'
'hey you up there
what are you hinting at
what's with that zeppelin milk?'
'you'd better go to a doctor who can
put your imagination in a cast'
'go to hell'
'get lost'
'mister, got a licence?!'
In the end I was forced to climb down.
Being young had become boring.

In the hospital five doctors gawked at my death
as through a windowpane.
One thumped on my chest.
I told him to come in even though I hadn't been
inhabiting myself for a while.
'So much the better,' he replied. 'We can rent you out.'
So I'm at your disposal –
cheap,
comfortable,
impatient to watch you throw dice for my orange shirt.

Nirvana

(In the south of India there grows a strange plant
whose leaves when chewed
allow a man to survive for sixteen days
without being hungry at all.)

Give us, oh Lord, our daily hunger
give us potato and onion,
the kitchens in which revolts have foundered,
our saliva in which gods mirror themselves.

Happy barbarian
at the outskirts of the empire
with his savage hand
picking marble grapes
from the cornice of the sacred temple.

Conversation

Learning that I write poetry
a painter in whom old age has shyly washed its feet
as if in a basin of hot water
(blessed simplicity – he was almost fifty, I mean)
offers to give me his raincoat
(out of fashion now but bought in Paris)
he's ready to pay for my beer
and my impertinence to boast of my genius
yet he swears at me patronisingly
(with a pair of tricolour skis
he has scaled High Society
but lacks the courage to come down)
yet he coughs in my face
with the warmth of a living classic
(what a time he had when he was the cubest of cubes)
and yet, and yet again,
what am I supposed to do
except to mistake his telephone number
for the bill,
and yet, and yet again,
what am I finally supposed to do
except shout,
'emotional algebra
constructive void
enfeebled aurora,
knock three times with your finger
at your mother's womb
and enter without waiting for a response.'

Myopic painter

Many a madman has imagined himself a general
and some have even become one,
the myopic decorator of Easter eggs may one day paint a church
and it's not impossible that a comet will later crash into its steeple
and cry out, 'Christ is risen'
just as you
who swear you love me
may once upon a time even come to love me.

Inventory of the fourth world

Those who before a war gargle with camomile tea
who chase butterflies with a ladle
who nibble away a martyr's halo
who enter churches with an organ in their belly
who pick their noses while others dig their graves
who flush the toilet lest their weeping be overheard
who dream of limousines but make do with just fries
who are delivered by an operation from their obsession with an angel
who ignore the aesthetics of force
the idealists the musical the shy
the word polishers
fail to see the city sail high into the air
and piss in the sea
as Mount Everest disembarks from a ship
with suitcases full of parachutists
as a flatiron hot with excitement
crushes a mouse
as neurotic forests amble towards sanatoriums
at the hour of petty compromises with people's happiness
when action feeds on song
when we die of applause.

Evolution of a dream

The winter holidays are approaching – where can we mirror
    ourselves
when spittoons have buried their brass under our merry bills
after the useful custom of the ostrich
who strives to know nothing?
I'm willing to go on letting myself be conned
yet I suspect that soon snow will be rationed,
I'm willing to consent to my sophisticated boredom
but the magi, parachuted into this city
as if heralding a film star's birth,
sell deluxe soap and paradise-infused cigarettes of perdition
on the black market.
And, behold, while waiting for the glory of the Void to turn rank
our cowardice has frozen it for eternity:
the dustman dreams he's a dustman
the honourable man he's honourable
the roundworm he's a roundworm.

The prodigal son's prayer

With a halo of little red flies above my head
here I stay vacillating between steamships and natives
sort of an official and lymphatic Rimbaud
it's not as if I'm longing to trade glass beads
for a wench
or to wrench a tongue of gold free for myself
I'd much rather take lessons in silence
from the lizard whose throat fan puffs out as big as a house.
Oh, the degradation of the species through happiness
all of a sudden small scales appear under my chin
and my adventure is depleted
between two butterflies that I eat with a smile,
but when aurora gathers
her bright raiment
I'll need to lisp my prayer,
'*O mio padre, mio fratello*,
if you can still recall the fair-haired child I once was
give up hunting tonight.'

Village with commuters

I've my own way of cheering up friends
with a bright red shirt smelling of fried fish
I slip inside the church and put a box of beer to chill
while the priest plays backgammon with the policeman
and *nouveau riche* gypsies dig a new groove in the gramophone
    record
because today's Monday Tuesday Wednesday Thursday Friday
    Saturday
that is to say a sort of slatternly Sunday
the dog's skin will soon be made into an accordion's bellows
and the fire extinguisher into a clandestine still for *ţuica*.
Towards evening
a train whistle at the far end of the village
leaves behind the overpowering smell of lavender and commuters
people who swear and laugh
whose faces I've never seen
I've no idea why the hell they're even here.

Apotheosis of the blind

The poet's craft is as profitable
as a bison hunt where the bison is extinct
that is to say you gnaw at butterfly bones
that is to say your photo is placed in a hungry tiger's cage
and while the tiger munches its scraps
two bullets come calling at your home
as a tribute from his dreamy eyes.

Scrape the children's smiles off your windowpanes
and consider death as a luxury for the poor.

The film of dawn is projected on your contorted face:
the aged teacher takes the kerosene can for a walk
in a pram
a woman combs her hair
and fiery banknotes fall from her head
(in their gleam her husband blanches white as a guinea pig
into which a rebellious scholar's brain has been transplanted)
electric whips drive happy youths
towards the song-shambles...

You can hear an apple rotting
in the ape's stomach
the priest wipes cinders off the Good Lord's halo
yesterday's dirty laundry
migrates like storks towards the sunlit subconscious.

Only the beloved woman's laughter keeps up such a strange chiming
that blind men's hands drop into hats
with excitement.

Night prayer

Sunday night
five drunk gypsies threatened a tram driver
with their knives and forced him
to race past stations without stopping,
as they were in a rush
to get to a much darker district:
'Why, God, haven't you brought an ocean liner
on our little Dâmboviţa
why have we no airport in Dudeşti
why keep us here, full of sour beer,
staring in humiliation at the fan blades
that turn round and round and round
on the ceiling of the pub
that we're about to hijack.'

Fiesta

Your beauty bursts my chest
bulls as light as jellyfish
rise over the city,
come,
while hope still jangles in my pockets
while spring hasn't razed its market stalls.

An umbrella of sparrows pops open
but rain forgets to pour down
the tower clock sticks out its tongue at passers-by
the newspapers read by the wind
announce a strike of kiwi birds
an insurrection of cacao trees
bulls are being washed under hot water jets in slaughterhouses
while you strangle roses with your handkerchief –
you blow into my love as into an antique lamp.

Fish

The gods' images vanished from
the food tins' labels eons ago,
there remain only a band of old people
who in the downpour pursue a church with a made-up face
while the sunflower's delicate machinery
rumbles endlessly on the hill.

We stand in the field men and cattle crowded together
and like elegant steamships
the sea's nerves no longer endure
seem to float across the green fields
leaving behind a slick of petrol and merrymaking.

Like shy fish under the floating paradise
we await the rope
that will hoist us on deck.

But there's no rope.
One world passes through another
and they never touch.

One day our great pity

One day our great pity
will move from the outskirts to the centre
where the angel brought on a stretcher from intensive care
is forced to do his duty on the cathedral steps.
You've the moral obligation to ignore your neighbour,
otherwise you'll have Bosnia and Herzegovina with you under your
    blankets,
or the unprejudiced woodpeckers
that already have devoured the Novosibirsk radar
will peck at your salaries,
otherwise you'll see the gold threads of the rabid dog's muzzle
in the bride's tiara
and the blood of the bespectacled Hungarian (world champion at
    suicide)
washed with hot-water jets from the snout of the Orient Express
behind the engine depot.
You'd better remember that you have a bow-legged aunt in America
and thus you're related by marriage to the Triumphal Arch,
you'll testify that when the black man wipes his mouth
a little soot is visible on the tissue,
but please
I beg you
for God's sake
don't make any more children with the aid of drugs
don't make any more children with the aid of drugs
I beg you
don't make any more children
because our great pity will move from the outskirts to the centre.

Chinoiserie

In the year 200 BC
the (Chinese) poet Li-Ber
peeled an orange
inside he found a tiny ballerina
who'd become lost in the woods
during the No-Tank dynasty.
In the year 1978
while eagerly peeling an orange
I was struck by the smell of mercury sulphate
and a little maggot
that had conquered its core
shouted angrily at me,
'Wretch, never again trust legends.'

Artist's life

I invented you
but now you share your beauty with everyone
like bread,
I invented you – but now I'm a mere hairpin
in your hair that presages autumn.
Once pet rabbits nested in you
you'd close your eyes and I'd feel sleepy
today I ride trams
I'm almost ashamed that I write poetry
and if I could pack my life in steamer trunks
I'd abandon them beyond the city limits
happy as a teenage bicyclist.
And look, as in a fairy tale the astrologer knocks
at my door to interpret the stars on the electric meter
reminding me I'm alive,
then comes the exacting accountant
likewise reminding me I'm alive,
but you never come
and it's as if my own silly smile in the mirror
shouts back at me instead of you, 'Live, you ninny! live...'

Tea

(for Gheorghe Pituţ)

There's always someone
who looks after me
(only by wearing dead men's clothes
could I escape that)
but the day must come when churches doff their steeples
and wish me 'good evening'
and my trumpet is buried in the earth
where despairingly I blow my love into stones...

P.S. Because the only thing left for us
was to scatter our poems to the wind,
I sat drinking tea with my friend at literature's farthest reach
calling ourselves editors of the spring monsoon,
until good hopes impelled us to go to the wheat field
at reaping
along with our typewriters
and this is how we paid for the tea – your tea or your life.

Cows

These cows flown here from Holland
are the pride of our county.
I swear
seven gypsies hired to serenade them softly
stay hidden among maize stalks till evening
the cowherds hiccup in the shower
offended and sneeze in the x-ray machine
and the doctor chides them because their clothes
stink of tobacco and plum brandy.
If it hadn't been for the blind villages everywhere around
and barefoot urchins in the pasture
staining the landscape
well surely these bovine ballerinas
would've won many more medals.

Cats of the Vatican

Glory unto you, cats of the Vatican,
here where autos and angels
dare not turn into forbidden streets
you ignore the early masses utopia and pride
and in the haze of fried potatoes
you leap about like barbarians at the fall of empires,
district comets,
streaks of lightning combed and pestered by rain

You who know just like the prophet
that only rebels live in dry places
at the hour when
high middle and low functionaries
with degrees in fear
would gladly escape into the green Africa of your pupils,
you blink your phosphorescent guillotine,
drowsily behead them from afar,
so the insufferable stench of passports
won't reach the rooftops.

Message from a shipwrecked sailor

If instead of the sun my dazzling
18-carat destiny would rise in the sky
you'd go on calmly
cultivating carrots for your soup
instead of love for your neighbour
arrogantly combing your women through your teeth
conceitedly disguising your mistakes with a peacock's tail
in the fog of my song you'll never notice
that I'm retreating into the empty wine bottle
like a message for future times
to wait for a ship
in this city
where the sea can no longer be found.

Letter to my mother

You tell me that rats have gnawed the church down to its roots
my sad mother
but even so our faith depends much more
on bread and wine,
if only the oats hadn't bent low to the ground
in the bed of my sister who fled into the field
if only the singer chased into the reeds hadn't grown wild
over death who combs your hair
high above the fire's entrails
storks fly like a leukaemia of the stars.

Rented sun

I'm an oily patch on the high windows
of your life that gets starched every day
neither force nor rain will make me vanish
just as a beggar's pocket change
attracts lightning
I'll slip a rat
killed in the garden by the watchmen
among the silver cutlery
and on the melon rind you'll find a poem
deliberately scratched there with my fingernail
here's a cleft in the wall
one of your daughters will elope through it with a poor student
but you'll take refuge under the cheaply rented sun
celebrating your indigestion,
let him bark, you say,
let him bark,
don't throw him even a bone as you used to
just stretch out calmly under the rays of my brilliant fangs.

Good evening

Ever since I was in the womb
my mother's arteries have welcomed
headstrong firing squads.

God pulled his hat down over his ears
instead of a halo he had a pressure cooker
you had to invoke him as 'Mr Bear'
so that in the thick of a great battle he could answer,
'I'm hibernating.'

Like rabbits out of the smuggler's top hat, heroes popped up
with the enthusiastic leap
of the decapitated.

I chose to be born
rather than be forced to,
lucifers can be struck on my tongue
I know so much
that some keep watch on my mouth
as if it were a talking stake on a pyre.

Otherwise, I'm like everybody else: I drink my tea tepid
I climb out three times a day to say good evening.

Screws

In spring dustmen pass with refuse bins
full of cranky children
who ask for a passage to the sea.
Surely they've as much need of sewer outlets
as the Venus de Milo of gloves,
because the only running water here
stinks and it mostly flows mornings and evenings
and besides it ends up in an open field.
Eventually we decide
that the sea is the invention of shirkers
so we screw the children back into place.

Between imagination and humility

They climbed up on the stake as into the evening mail coach
God would be waiting at the next station disguised
as an innkeeper,
everything was free: entertainment – death,
friends kept bringing a generous supply of firewood...

Travelling in the south of food tins
with the inquisition in my blood like a heretic for hire
in the sweet steam of soup cured of revolt
now I'm still nostalgic for the dusty provincial train
that chugs 'good evening' as it crosses my kitchen,
the very train I used to throw
onions at,
a slow train, local and 'personal', as if it belonged to me,
a pitiful train that coughed between stations,
the train for whose sake I myself would chew coal
between imagination and humility
hesitating hesitating hesitating.

So?!

Let me have my own way with a provincial newspaper
a wooden booth and a dirty signboard
three days later the cities will reek of vanilla
and free ports.

Absurd chess

Sweet naivety
to suppose that poetry can bring about a better world.
It's like tossing a lump of sugar
to a tiger in a cage
and expecting it at once to read Shakespeare.
Bloated by your own disaster
(as if you'd lunched in the mirror)
you hiss like a train at the station
until the crowd crushes you underfoot
hurrying to claim the warm spot on your nape.
Since dream is the bastard child
of reality,
remember that absurd chess match
in which the madman moved villages
first sacrificing the horses under the knights
and a thousand comrades rushed to praise his game.

Monologue with a mouse

In order to reach the castle
I climb into a decrepit car
that moves as if powered by an accordion bellows
pumped up by the gypsies' hilarity.
In their gaze
a marginal civilisation decants strong contempt.
The knife never asks your name,
sour wine and the smell of manure on boots
give swear words the sound of domestic familiarity.
Their poverty isn't at all frightening
(proof is in the low flight of the stork seeking its nest)
they've no church because they know all there is to know about
        one another,
fascinated like rabbits
in the blinding light of crime
they take the time to fling throughout the city
handfuls of noisy children.
I live in a kind of kitchen in a real castle,
I'm a ridiculous guy: I wheel images around in a wheelbarrow,
I catch a mouse in my cap because I want to talk to it
and it dies of a heart attack because it can't stand
my love or my boredom
my loneliness or my song.

Bulldozer

What use are friends
when one morning so bored that you turn the knob for the gas
to heat water for tea
and with the match to light it in your hand
you hesitate
suddenly toying with death?
Friends always face cancer with a bag of oranges
they speak well of you for a long time
sometimes they shatter a glass in memoriam
donate a pint of blood
that they throw in your face at the next drinking party
they'll lose your image in a field of sugar cane
until the cancer proves not to be cancer
and wonder fades to disillusionment
your recovery begins to appear to you dubious and in bad taste
and what moves you from then on
what really moves you
won't be either the ticking of the clock
or music
or liberty
but only the bulldozer
that rams your chair.

Hypothetical transhumance

I beg you, lead me now
to the donkey asylum in the south of England,
porridge is sure to be sweet there,
and I can walk my paper skeleton,
my delicate lady-like bones,
across the meadows without fear of censorship.
When old millionaires scratch me
between the ears and offer me a borsch,
or their foil-wrapped kids
rub my gums with sugar candy,
don't worry – I won't say a word,
I'll be as silent as I am in Romania.

Sign hunter

At the end of tramline 6
radiant gypsy girls sell poison mushrooms
a shoeshine boy reads the life of Napoleon
the artist is nothing more than the paralytic barber's customer
but the cognac distillery looms high above all
its aluminium humiliates the church
plastic barrels gleam like icons
water dresses itself up as wine
it must be that God's in the pipes
the magi, guided by x-rays,
knock on your chest as on the door of a sanatorium.
Pretend you haven't heard
spring's on its way
otherwise where have these foxes stained by diesel oil come from
these bookkeepers with carrots up their arses
sneaking towards the carob-tree forest?

Far below
at the Danube's mouth
clickety clickety a sewing machine busies itself patching moorhens
     and pelicans
or maybe it's the echo of rifle shots?
Pretend you haven't heard spring's on its way,
and the city's dull roar dries all tears:
the small explosion of a thread in the tights on the girl's calves
the soldier's shouting in the tiny station
the faint squeak of the mouse starving in the post box
the laughter of movers crouched on top of their lorries with a load
     of cheap furniture.

Impoverished biography

Some people can't wait to see me floating
like Ophelia with coronets of newspapers,
but too much imagination exhausts them
they enter my biography solemnly as if a leper colony
ready to identify the white patches and call out,
danger of contamination
musical virus
bacteria burdened with teardrops
a dog with residual effects
his eyes gaping wide at the golden hams of the West
he claims he's not hungry
he sings foolishly like a jukebox that rejects coins
in the engine depot his father stealthily sniffs the lavender
his mother hauls crates and grows deaf (we suspect it's that she doesn't
    want to hear)
his sister teaches at a school for retarded children and feels truly free
no one knows anything about his brother and that's much more
    worrisome
the existence of this family predisposes him to tolerance
but he loves his country in a rather unusual way
that troubles us
and we can't remove the sweet earth from his mouth
without the churches of his native land crumbling.

The moles

In the evening, the old men's heels
rustle like dry yellowed newspapers.
What else can we do? They whisper
about the prisons they've been in,
of leather, of rubber, of hemp.
They weren't born blind –
under rosy eyelids they contemplated
an infantile mountain nibbled at by conjectural goats,
brass bands from before World War I
slurping food from the biggest ladle.
In darkness and sweat,
the return tunnel has caved in.
Five tears with blunt nails
trickle down
from the eyes of the horn-hard moles.

Death and the cat

The cat alone understands what the stove's roar tells us,
she goes out and whispers the tale to the rattling flue,
then she deciphers the hieroglyphs of a little mouse,
yawns a great big yawn
swallowing the house, the steeple, the entire district.
Then she opens her eyes and reinvents everything.
Only the priest gets delayed in her yellow pupils:
he went to check whether by mistake he'd locked
some old woman in the church.

The disappearance of the mountain

Hereabouts the peasants are used to
drinking liqueur made out of the oranges from the potassium
        factory.
In truth, when the wind shears the sheep
and the shepherd loses his proud moustache
because of acid rain,
a grove of orange trees seems to shuttle
on caterpillar tracks of yellowish smoke
between one village and the next.
At night you can bargain with watchmen,
a twenty for a bucket of methyl alcohol.
Across the Danube, at Ruse, Bulgarians
keep a fearful eye on the Romanian clouds
from which gravediggers derive good profit,
and doctors are greeted in the street
much more respectfully than before.

Long ago only rumours about Huns
who knowing nothing about potatoes or corn
were content to bake babies on hot ashes
could make them pack their junk and rags in bundles
and large raffia baskets,
chubby children on one side
of the donkey,
the precious onions on the other,
and trade the mud that bore golden fruit
for the lime in mountain strongholds.
Now their lives are transformed by clouds
(courtesy of the Romanian chemical industry)
that send them migrating towards a mountain
already worn down, almost flat, illusory,
whose high peaks are still preserved today
only in ancient songs.

House search

They methodically prised up the parquet,
unscrewed the light fixtures,
whispered in the wardrobe,
gave lectures in the fridge,
tore the pillows apart,
shot up the walls,
but they never found the Siberian ape
swinging gaily from lobe to lobe
in my tropical brain.

Trip

In order to bring art out into the street
don't resort to the dilapidated lift
so many shady deals have been planned in...
First of all renounce poetry
and you'll have many fewer stomach aches.
You can prolong your life by means of cynicism
you can replace a word by an anecdote
you can stick your tongue out at the sun like a first edition
you can move the Eiffel Tower into a cellar
(just file off a few grams a day).
Suicide no longer pays the rent.
In order to become a celebrated European writer
you've got to be a cannibal at least,
or suggest a wacky proposal for making the Sahara bloom
(for instance, parachuting there
everybody with water on the lungs).
Passive madmen are not in demand:
if you married a meat grinder
some American trust
might pay for your honeymoon trip
provided you extrude spicy tasteless children
identical to their famous hamburger...
Consumer society humiliates you with melons in winter
and in summer you carry eggs in your down jacket
for the Metropolitan Opera soloists.
You doze on the banks of the Seine
and suddenly you smell the Dâmboviţa,
like a spooked provincial
you hope that if you meander down a little street in Montparnasse
you'll happen upon Bucharest.
It's not easy for you to understand
that poetry no longer needs paper
that a bullet makes itself heard more clearly than a book

that dentists mechanics hairdressers pilots
waiters engineers tycoons admirals and gazillionaire dustmen
naturally never feel inclined to read sonnets,
because life's primary aim is to relate to the fat in the soup
that always floats on top.

Poet's confession

For a long time I believed that poetry slept under a heron's wing
or that I'd have to dig it out in a forest
but like a prophet driven from the desert by the gurgling of oil wells,
I'm now ready to come to terms with reality
and admit I was wrong:
I'll smash this wall with a pickaxe
to let you peer in.

Artist left out in the rain

Doubtless there exists a grammar of the wall
with the door necessarily set mid-sentence
through which the much-pitied author enters
to proclaim that the revolution has swept away the grand themes
and now what's left for him is only
to tell about the adventure of a mouthful of bread
as it descends through the gullet
like the hero of a Greek tragedy
confronted by noxious gastric juices
or about the sadness of the cake left out in the rain
to swell crumble burst apart.
Shhh!
Quiet please.
Behind the curtain
the critic
with a jeweller's scales
is weighing the snot on Desdemona's handkerchief.

THE TRANSLATORS

Lidia Vianu, a poet, novelist, critic, and translator, is Professor of Modernist and Contemporary British Literature at the University of Bucharest, where she is also Director of the publishing house Contemporary Literature Press (http://mttlc.ro) and of the eZine *Translation Café*. She has been Fulbright professor at the University of California Berkeley and SUNY Binghamton. Vianu has published over 20 books of literary criticism, including *The AfterMode* and *T.S. Eliot: An Author for All Seasons*. She has also published several English learning manuals, and has translated over 70 books into English and Romanian, including two translated with Adam J. Sorkin and published by Bloodaxe, Marin Sorescu's *The Bridge* (2004), winner of the 2005 Corneliu M. Popescu Prize for European Poetry Translation, and Mircea Dinescu's *The Barbarians' Return* (2018). She has published both in Romania and abroad: see *Censorship in Romania* (Central European University Press, 1997).

Adam J. Sorkin translates contemporary Romanian poetry. His work has won Poetry Society, Ioan Flora Foundation and Poesis Translation prizes, as well as support from the Fulbright, Rockefeller and Soros Foundations, the Academy of American Poets, Arts Council England, Romanian Cultural Institute, and the U.S. National Endowment for the Arts. Sorkin has published four translations of Romanian poets with Bloodaxe: Liliana Ursu's *The Sky Behind the Forest* (translated with Ursu and Tess Gallagher), Ioana Ieronim's *The Triumph of the Water Witch* (with Ieronim), Marin Sorescu's *The Bridge* (with Lidia Vianu), winner of the 2005 Corneliu M. Popescu Prize for European Poetry Translation, and Mircea Dinescu's *The Barbarians' Return* (2018). His recent books include *The Hunchbacks' Bus* by Nora Iuga (Bitter Oleander Press, translated with Diana Manole), *Syllables of Flesh* by Floarea Țuțuianu (Plamen Press, with Irma Giannetti), and *A Deafening Silence* by Magda Cârneci (Shearsman Books, with Mădălina Bănucu and the author). Sorkin is Distinguished Professor Emeritus, Penn State University.

MIX
Paper from responsible sources
FSC
www.fsc.org
FSC® C007785